TYPE 2 DIABETES MEAL PREP COOKBOOK FOR BEGINNERS

MARY LEE

Table of Contents

INTRODUCTION

Nutritional management of the blood glucose levels remains the strategic target in the prevention and management of type 2 diabetes mellitus, to implement such a tactic it is very crucial to understand the impact of dietary components on blood glucose levels.

Blood glucose is a sugar which the bloodstream transport to all body cells to supply them with energy. We get obtain this sugar from diet most especially carbohydrates. The body monitor the blood glucose levels so that they remain in a normal healthy range; sufficient to fuel the body however not in excess in the bloodstream.

The internal environment of the blood must be stable to sustain the vital body functions. When a person takes in carbohydrates through diet, it is broken down into glucose which serve as the major source of energy. However, glucose only get into the cells of the body if there is sufficient insulin in the bloodstream. Insulin is a hormone that takes glucose into the cells. the cells would starve without sufficient insulin as the case of type 1 diabetes or if they become resistance to its effect in type 2 diabetes thereby causing hyperglycemia or high blood glucose, a symptom that characterizes diabetes.

Type 2 diabetes mellitus is a chronic disease characterized by a condition called insulin resistance, in which the body cannot use the insulin produced effectively to transport blood sugar to cells and muscles for energy which if left untreated can lead to severe health complications such as cardiovascular diseases, kidney diseases, loss of vision etc.

Type 2 diabetes is the most common type of diabetes, more than 95% of persons diagnosed of diabetes have type 2. People who are middle-aged or older are most likely to have this kind of diabetes, however it affects kids and teenagers now mainly due to childhood obesity. It is believed that type 2 diabetes have a strong link to genetics, implying that it tends to run in the families. However, obesity and inactive lifestyle are the two major common causes of it.

Diabetes is one of the diseases that the management mainly depend on the individual. Making changes to your lifestyle through diet, weight control and physical activities. In fact, evidence have shown that many people who lose weight and adopt a low-carbohydrate diet can control their blood glucose levels enough to be able to reduce or even stop their medication. The food you eat every day plays crucial role in management of diabetes as well as ensuring that you keep well and have enough energy for your daily activities.

In truth, following a diabetes diet does not mean you will give up in eating your favorite meals and special family means. A diet aimed at lowering the risk of diabetes is really nothing more than a nutritionally balanced diets that support maintenance of blood glucose levels at a healthy range and ensure weight loss as weight is a sensitive issue for many people, however there are huge benefits of losing weight if you have extra weight. It helps to lower the risk of health issues such as heart disease and stroke and helps in controlling diabetes.

The same healthy-eating habits apply if you have diabetes or not. In fact, getting the whole family to eat this sort of balanced diet if you have diabetes can benefit their health as well as yours.

EASY AND DELICIOUS RECIPES TO MANAGE AND EVEN REVERSE DIABETES

DIABETIC APPETIZER RECIPES

BLACK BEAN HUMMUS WITHOUT TAHINI

Servings: 8

Ingredients:

- Fifteen ounces of no-salt-added black beans (drained and rinsed)
- One-fourth cup of fresh cilantro
- One-fourth cup of lime juice

- One tablespoon of sesame oil
- One jalapeno pepper (trimmed and seeded)
- Four cloves garlic
- One teaspoon of ground cumin
- One-fourth teaspoon of ground paprika
- One-fourth teaspoon of cayenne pepper

Directions

- Mix black beans, cilantro, lime juice, jalapeno pepper, sesame oil, garlic cumin, paprika and cayenne pepper in a blender and blend until smooth.

VEGAN GRANOLA BARS

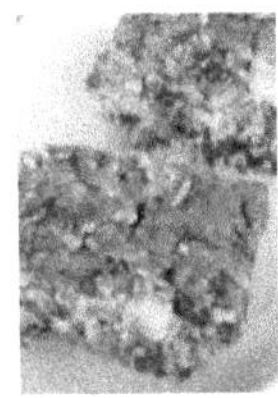

Servings: 9

Ingredients:

- One and half cups of rolled oats
- One cup of raisins

- One chopped raw almond
- One-fourth cup of unsalted raw peanut butter
- Half teaspoon of vanilla extract
- One pinch of salt
- One tablespoon of water (not compulsory)
- One banana

Directions

- Pulse raisins into paste, in a food processor.
- Put the paste in a bowl and put oats and almonds.
- Blend banana into a puree in the food processor.
- Mix one-fourth cup of banana puree, peanut butter, vanilla extract and salt in the saucepan over medium heat. For about five minutes, cook and turn until it warms through. Put water if the mixture is too thick. Transfer over raisin mixture in the bowl and use hands to mix well.
- Use parchment paper to line a square baking dish. Press mixture

into the baking dish. Brush remaining banana puree over. Use plastic wrap to cover.

- Chill for about eight hours or overnight until firm then cut into squares.

PINEAPPLE SALSA

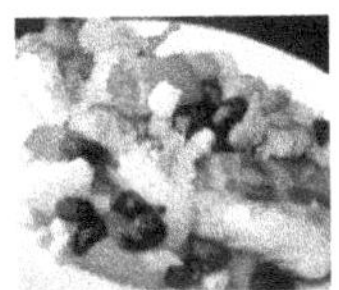

Servings: 8

Ingredients:

- Half cup of diced red bell pepper
- Half cup of diced green bell pepper
- One cup of finely chopped fresh pineapple
- One cup of frozen corn kernels (thawed)
- Fifteen ounces of black beans (drained and rinsed)
- One-fourth cup of chopped onions
- Two green chile peppers (chopped)
- One-fourth cup of orange juice

- One-fourth cup of chopped fresh cilantro
- Half teaspoon of ground cumin
- Salt and pepper to taste

Directions

- Toss pineapple, red bell pepper, green bell pepper, corn, black beans, onions, green chile peppers, orange juice and cilantro in a big bowl.
- Use cumin, salt and pepper to season. Cover and chill in the refrigerator until when you want to serve.

SPICED SWEET ROASTED RED PEPPERS HUMMUS

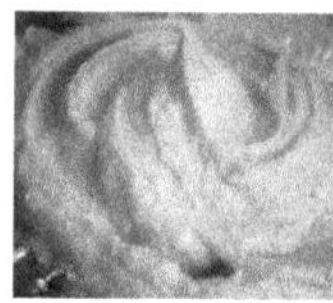

Servings: 8

Ingredients:

- Four ounces of roasted red peppers

- Fifteen ounces of garbanzo beans (drained)
- Three tablespoons of lemon juice
- One and half tablespoons of tahini
- One clove garlic (minced)
- Hal teaspoon of cayenne pepper
- Half teaspoon of ground cumin
- One-fourth teaspoon of salt
- One tablespoon of chopped fresh parsley

Directions

- Puree the chickpeas, red peppers, lemon juice, garlic, tahini, cumin, cayenne and salt in a blender. Use long pulses to process until the mixture is smooth. As you blend, ensure that you scrape the mixture off the sides of the blender.
- Pour in a serving bowl and for not less than an hour, refrigerate.
- Sprinkle chopped parsley over the hummus before you serve.

MIKI`S JICAMA

Servings: 32

Ingredients:

- Two jicamas (peeled and diced)
- Twelve plum tomatoes (diced)
- One red onion (diced)
- Four poblano peppers (diced)
- Six jalapeno peppers (seeded and diced)
- Three tablespoons of chopped garlic
- Four limes (juiced)
- One-fourth cup of chopped fresh cilantro
- Three tablespoons of white balsamic vinegar
- One-fourth cup of salt

Directions

- Toss together diced tomatoes, jicamas. Poblano peppers, red onions and jalapeno peppers with garlic, lime juice, cilantro, white balsamic vinegar and salt in a big mixing bowl.

APPLE LADYBUG TREATS

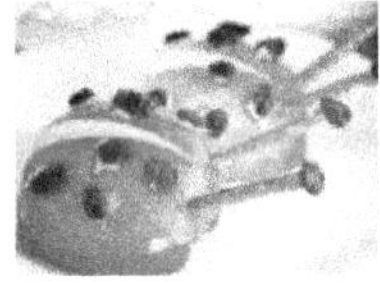

Servings: 4

Ingredients:

- Two red apples
- One tablespoon of peanut butter
- One-fourth cup of raisins
- Eight thin pretzel sticks

Directions

- Cut apples in half from top to bottom. With a knife, ladle out the cores. You can core them first using apple corer and then slice. Keep each apple half flat side down on a plate.
- Dab peanut butter on to the lady bug`s back, stick raisin onto the dabs for spots. With this method, make the eyes. Stick one end of each pretzel stick into a raisin and

then press the other end into the apples to form the antennae.

SMOKED SALSA

Servings: 8

Ingredients:

- Two onions (diced)
- Four tomatoes (diced)
- One green bell pepper (diced)
- One red bell pepper (diced)
- One orange bel pepper (diced)
- One yellow bell pepper (diced)
- Three jalapeno peppers (diced)
- One lime (juiced)
- Salt and ground black pepper to taste
- One-fourth teaspoon of garlic powder
- One bunch of fresh cilantro (chopped)

Directions

- Preheat a smoker grill to (250 degrees Fahrenheit). According to the manufacturer`s directions, put wood chips.
- Mix tomatoes, onions, bell peppers and jalapeno peppers in an aluminum grill pan. Keep on the grate of the smoker grill and for about three hours, smoke.
- Take the vegetables away from the smoker and keep in a blender. Blend to desired consistency. Combine in the lime juice, garlic powder, salt and pepper. Put fresh cilantro for decoration.

DIABETIC MAIN RECIPES

CHICKEN FIESTA SALAD

Servings: 4

Ingredients:

- Two skinless, boneless chicken breast halves
- One tablespoon of vegetables oil
- Fifteen ounces of black beans (rinsed and drained)
- One packet of dry fajita seasoning (divided)
- Eleven ounces of Mexican-style corn
- One onion (chopped)
- One tomato (slice into wedges)
- Ten ounces of mixed salad greens

Directions

- ➢ Use half of the fajita seasoning to rub the chicken evenly. Over medium heat, heat oil in a skillet. For about ten minutes, cook the chicken on each side or until juices run clear. Keep it aside.
- ➢ Combine beans, corn, salsa and the remaining half of the fajita seasoning in a big saucepan. Over medium heat, heat until it gets warm.

- Prepare salad by tossing the onions, tomato and greens. Add the chicken over salad and dress with the beans and corn mixture.

SPICY STEAMED SHRIMP

Servings: 2

Ingredients:

- One pound of tiger prawns with shell
- One quart of water
- Three ounces of old bay seasoning
- Twelves ounces of jar cocktail sauce

Directions

- In a pot, bring one quart of water to a boil.
- Keep shrimp in a steamer basket and keep over the pot and then cover. Don't immerse shrimp. Remove some water if possible. Season the shrimp with old bay seasoning.

- Steam the shrimp until it is pink.
- Remove the shell while you eat dipping in cocktail sauce.

AIR FRYER FALAFEL

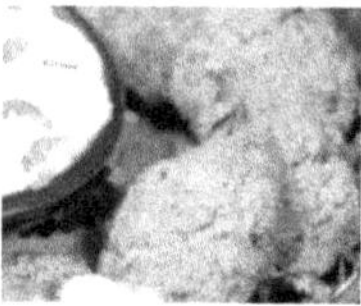

Servings: 15

Ingredients:

- One and half cups of fresh cilantro (stems removed)
- One cup of dry garbanzo beans
- Three-quarter cup of fresh flat-leafed parsley (stems removed)
- One clove garlic
- One small red onion (quartered)
- Two tablespoons of chickpea flour
- One tablespoon of sriracha sauce
- One tablespoon of ground cumin
- One tablespoon of ground coriander
- Salt and ground black pepper to taste
- Half teaspoon of baking powder

- Cooking spray
- One-fourth teaspoon of baking soda

Directions

- For about a day, soak chickpeas in a large quantity of cool water. Lose and remove the skins by rubbing the soaked chickpeas with your finger. Rinse and drain completely. On a large clean dish towel, spread the chickpeas to dry.
- In a blender, blend chickpeas, cilantro, onion, parsley and garlic until a rough paste form. Pour the mixture into a bowl. Put chicken flour, coriander, cumin, sriracha, salt and pepper, then mix well. Cover the bowl and allow the mixture rest for about an hour.
- Preheat an air fryer to (375 degrees Fahrenheit).
- Put baking powder and baking soda to the chickpea mixture. Use hands to mix until it combines well. Create fifteen equal-sized balls and press slightly to form

patties. Use cooking spray and spray falafel patties.

- Keep seven falafel patties in the already set air fryer and cook for up to ten minutes. Remove the cooked falafel and put on a plate, then cook the remaining eight falafels.

PUFFY TACO SHELLS

Servings: 4

Ingredients:

- Half teaspoon of kosher salt
- One cup of masa harina
- Half cup of lukewarm water
- Half cup of canola oil (for frying)
- Two tablespoons of lukewarm water

Directions

- With fingertips, combine together masa harina, salt and half cup plus two tablespoons of water in a bowl until dough forms and pull away from the sides. Make a firm, flattened ball and divide it into eight equal portions. Roll each portion into a ball. Cover dough balls using a damp paper towel as you fry them one after the other.

- Keep dough ball between two sheets of plastic. Flatten to make a small circle about (1/8-inch).
- Over medium heat, heat oil in a skillet. Once hot, slide in the first circle. Baste hot oil over the top of the shell carefully using a spoon to keep oil circulating on top surface. Once the shell puffs after about fifteen to twenty seconds, cook for some seconds further and turn it over to cook for about thirty seconds. Use slotted spoon to remove it and drain on paper towels. Repeat the procedure for the remaining shell.
- Carefully push down puffed tops to make room for filings when the shells are still warm and pliable,

then crease the shells slightly for folding.

- Fill with favorite taco fixings and serve while the shells are still hot.

OVERNIGHT LIGHT PB&J OATS

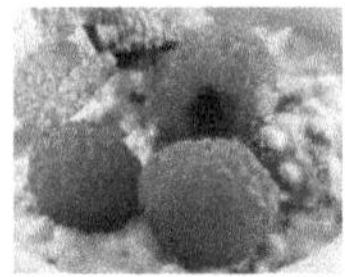

Servings: 1

Ingredients:

- On-fourth cup of fresh raspberries
- Half cup of almond milk
- One-fourth cup of rolled oats
- Two tablespoons of powered peanut butter
- One teaspoon of white sugar
- One and half teaspoons of chia seeds

Directions

- Combine almond milk, raspberries, rolled oats, powered peanut butter, chia, seeds and sugar together in a container. Cover and refrigerate until oats are tender, for eight hours to overnight.

SKINNY CHICKEN TACOS

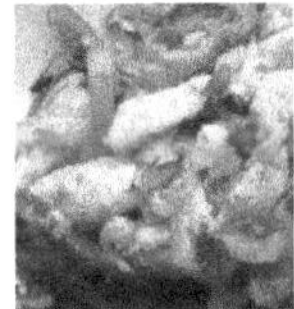

Servings: 4

Ingredients:

- Three limes (juiced and divided)
- Two teaspoons of ground cumin (divided)
- One pound of thinly sliced chicken breasts (cut into thin strips)
- Two tablespoons of garlic powder (divided)
- Two teaspoons of ground chipotle pepper (divided)
- One red onion (thinly sliced)
- Two red bell peppers (cut into thin strips)
- One bunch of cilantro (chopped)
- Four multi-grain tortillas or more to taste

- Two jalapeno peppers (stemmed, seeded and thinly sliced)

Directions

- ➢ Mix chicken, juice of one lime, one teaspoon of cumin, one teaspoon of garlic powder and one teaspoon of chipotle pepper in a bowl. Let it marinate for about ten minutes.
- ➢ In a big non-stick skillet, saute red bell peppers, onion, jalapeno peppers, juice of one lime, one teaspoon of cumin, one teaspoon of garlic powder and one teaspoon of chipotle pepper. Heat vegetables until soft and yet crispy for about four minutes over medium-high heat.
- ➢ Put the chicken mixture in another non-stick skillet over medium high-heat, saute until chicken is no longer pink in the middle, about eight minutes,
- ➢ Layer tortillas between paper towels on microwave-safe. Heat in microwave until it is warm, about twenty seconds.

- Ladle vegetables and chicken onto tortillas and add cilantro and lime juice on top.

CAPE MALAY PICKLED FISH

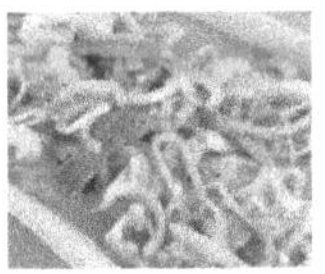

Servings: 6

Ingredients:

- Three pounds of cod fillets (cut into 2 to 3 ounce portions)
- Salt to taste
- Half cup of vegetable oil (for frying)
- Two large onions (peeled and cut into rings)
- Two cloves garlic (chopped)
- Eight whole black peppercorns
- Three bay leaves
- Four whole allspices berries
- One red chile pepper (seeded and sliced lengthwise)
- Half cup of water
- Two cups of red wine vinegar

- Half cup of packed brown sugar or to taste
- Two tablespoons of curry powder
- One teaspoon of ground turmeric
- Two teaspoons of ground coriander
- Two teaspoons of ground cumin

Directions

- Over medium-high heat, heat the oil in a large skillet. Season the fish with salt and keep in the skillet. For up to five minutes, fry each side until fish turns brown and done. Bring out from the skillet and keep aside.
- In the same skillet, fry the onions and garlic over medium heat until translucent. Put the peppercorns, allspice berries, bay leaves and red chile pepper. Add in the vinegar and water then bring to a boil. Add in the brown sugar until dissolved. Season with curry powder, turmeric, cumin and coriander.
- In a serving dish, layer pieces of fish and the pickling mixture. Add

the liquid over until the top layer is covered. Let cool then cover. For at least twenty-four hours, refrigerate before you serve.

SWEET POTATO-TURKEY MEATLOAF

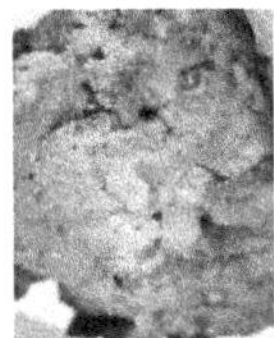

Servings: 4

Ingredients:

- One pound of ground turkey breast
- One large sweet potato (peeled and cubed)
- One small sweet onion (finely chopped)
- One egg
- One tablespoon of salt or to taste
- Two cloves garlic (minced)
- One tablespoon of freshly ground black pepper
- One small sweet onion (finely chopped)

- One-fourth cup of honey barbecue sauce
- One-fourth cup ketchup
- Two tablespoons of Dijon mustard
- Two slices whole-wheat bread, torn into small crumb

Directions

- Preheat oven to (350 degrees Fahrenheit). Grease a 2-quart baking dish lightly.
- Bring a pot with lightly salted water to a boil. Put the sweet potato and cook until tender for ten minutes. Drain the sweet potatoes and crush until smooth.
- Combine together the ground turkey with the egg, sweet onion, garlic, barbecue sauce, ketchup, Dijon mustard and whole wheat bread crumbs in a bowl. Add salt and pepper to season to taste. Put sweet potatoes and turn until combined. Put more bread crumbs if the mixture is too wet. Form the turkey mixture into a loaf shape

using hand. Keep in the prepared baking dish.

- For one hour, bake in the preheated oven. Slice the loaf and serve.

VENISON TIPS AND RICE

Servings: 4

Ingredients:

- One pound of venison stew meat
- One tablespoon of vegetable oil
- One green bell pepper (seeded and sliced into strips)
- One small onion (chopped)
- One red bell pepper (seeded and sliced into strips)
- One package of beef flavored rice mix (6.8 ounce)

Directions

- Over medium-high heat, heat oil in the skillet. Put the venison chunks and cook until it turns brown on the outside and almost done.

- Following the package directions, prepare the beef flavored rice mix. Put venison, green pepper, red pepper and onion while the rice cooks. Simmer until rice is cooked through and peppers soft.

INSTANT POT APPLE PIE STEEL CUT OATS

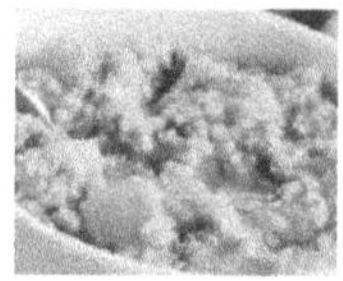

Servings: 4

Ingredients:

- One cup of steel-cut oats
- Three cups of water
- Half teaspoon of salt
- One apple or more to taste (chopped)
- One and half teaspoons of ground cinnamon
- One-fourth teaspoon of ground nutmeg

Directions

- In a multi-functional pressure cooker such as instant pot, mix water, oats, apple, cinnamon. Salt and nutmeg. Close the lid. Seal vent and choose manual function. Set timer for five minutes. Permit ten to fifteen minutes for pressure to build.
- For about ten minutes, using the natural release method according to manufacturer`s instruction, release pressure. Naturally release the remaining pressure. Stir and carefully remove the pot with the oven mitts.

SOUP AND STEW RECIPES

VEGGIE VEGETARIAN CHILI

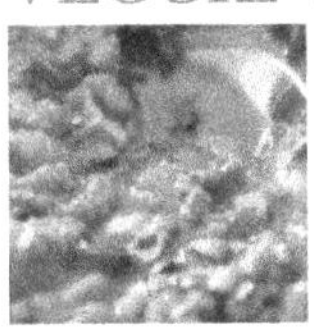

Servings: 16

Ingredients:

- Three cloves garlic (minced)
- One tablespoon of vegetable oil
- One cup of chopped green bell pepper
- One cup of chopped red bell pepper
- One cup of chopped onion
- One cup of chopped carrots
- One can of whole peeled tomatoes with liquid (twenty-eight ounces, chopped)
- One and half cups of chopped fresh mushrooms
- Two tablespoons of chili powder
- Fifteen ounces of black beans (undrained)
- Fifteen ounces of kidney beans (undrained)
- One tablespoon of cumin
- Fifteen ounces of whole kernel corn (drained)
- Fifteen ounces of pinto beans (undrained)
- One and half tablespoons of dried oregano

- One and half tablespoons of dried basil
- Half tablespoon of garlic powder

Directions

- Over medium heat, heat the oil in a pot. Cook and turn the garlic, onion and carrots in the pot until soft. Combine in the green bell pepper and red bel pepper. Season with chili powder. Keep on cooking for more five minutes or until peppers are soft.
- Combine the mushrooms into the pot. Add in the tomatoes with liquid, black beans with liquid, kidney beans with liquid, pinto beans with liquid and corn. Season with cumin, oregano, basil and garlic powder, then bring to a boil. Lower the heat to medium, cover and for about eighteen minutes, cook, turning it from time to time.

BEAN SOUP WITH KALE

Servings: 8

Ingredients:

- One yellow onion (chopped)
- One tablespoon of olive oil or canola oil
- Eight garlic cloves (minced)
- Four cups of chopped raw kale
- Four cups of low-fat, low-sodium chicken or vegetable broth
- Fifteen ounces of white beans such as cannellini or navy (undrained)
- Salt and pepper to taste
- One cup of chopped parsley
- Two teaspoons of dried Italian herb seasoning
- Four plum tomatoes (chopped)

Directions

- ➢ Heat oil in a pot. Put garlic and onion and saute until tender. Put kale and saute, turning until it wilts. Put three cups of broth, two cups of beans and all the tomatoes, herbs, salt and pepper. For about five minutes, simmer.

- Pour the remaining beans and broth in a blender, mix until smooth. Add into soup to thicken. For up to fifteen minutes, simmer. Spoon into bowls and sprinkle chopped parsley.

MANHATTAN CLAM CHOWDER

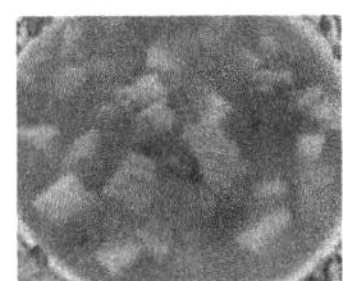

Servings: 8

Ingredients:

- Two potatoes (cleaned and chopped)
- One cup of tomato and clam juice cocktail
- One pint of shucked clams
- One-fourth cup of chopped green onions
- One cup of chopped green bell pepper
- One-fourth teaspoon of ground black pepper
- One can of Italian-style diced tomatoes

Directions

- Chop clams and reserve the juice. Keep the clams aside. Strain the clam juice to take away the bits of shell. Measure juice, put sufficient water to equal one and half cups of liquid.
- Mix clam juice mixture, clam-tomato juice cocktail, potatoes, bell peppers, scallions and black pepper in a saucepan. Heat to a boil. Lower the heat, cover and for about fifteen minutes, simmer or until potatoes are soft.
- Add in the undrained tomatoes and the chopped clans, then heat through.

SEAFOOD GUMBO STOCK

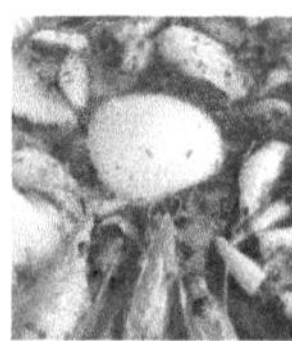

Servings: 8

Ingredients:

- Five quarts of water
- Shells from one of pound shrimp

- Four carrots (sliced)
- Four onions (quartered)
- Two bay leaves
- Half bunch of celery (sliced)
- Three cloves garlic (sliced)
- Five whole cloves
- Two sprigs of fresh parsley
- One tablespoon of dried basil
- Two teaspoons of dried thyme
- One teaspoon of ground black pepper

Directions

- At (375 degrees Fahrenheit), bake the shrimp shells until it dry and begin to turn brown on the edges.
- Mix water, carrots, onions, celery, bay leaves, garlic, parsley, cloves, pepper, basil, thyme and shrimp in an 8-quart pot. Bring to a boil slowly.
- Lower the heat and for six and half to seven hours, cook. Pour more water down the inside of the pot as needed.
- Bring the stock out of the heat and strain. Press all liquid from the

shells and vegetables and then discard them. Bring the liquid to heat, and lower to 2 to 3 quarts or to taste.

SPICY CHICKEN AND SWEET POTATO STEW

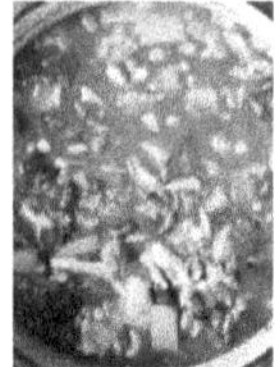

Servings: 6

Ingredients:

- Four cloves garlic (minced)
- One pound of sweet potato (peeled and cubed)
- One onion (chopped)
- One teaspoon of olive oil
- One orange bell pepper (seeded and cubed)
- One pound of cooked chicken breast (cubed)
- Two cups of water
- Twenty-eight ounces of diced tomatoes
- One teaspoon of salt

- Two tablespoons of chili powder
- One teaspoon of ground cumin
- One teaspoon of dried oregano
- One teaspoon of cocoa powder
- One-fourth teaspoon of ground cinnamon
- One-fourth teaspoon of red peppers flakes
- One and half tablespoons of all-purpose flour
- One cup of frozen corn
- Two tablespoons of water
- Sixteen ounces of kidney beans (rinsed and drained)
- Half cup of chopped fresh cilantro

Directions

- Over medium heat, heat olive oil in a pot. Add in onion and garlic; for about five minutes, cook and turn until onion are tender and translucent.
- Add in sweet potato, bell pepper, chicken, tomatoes and two cups of water. Season with salt, chili powder, cumin, oregano, cocoa

powder, cinnamon and red pepper flakes.

- Raise the heat to medium-high and bring to a boil. Put flour in two tablespoons of water and pour into the boiling stew. Lower the heat to medium-low, cover and then for about fifteen minutes, simmer until potatoes are soft but not mushy. Turn the stew from time to time to prevent it from sticking.
- When the potatoes are cooked, add in corn and kidney beans. For some minutes, cook until hot and then add in cilantro before you serve.

GOOD VEGGIE CHILI

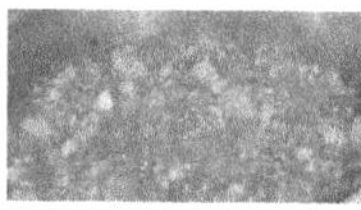

Servings: 8

Ingredients:

- One cup of water
- One onion (chopped)

- Half cup of texturized vegetable protein
- Two and half tablespoons of olive oil
- Six cloves garlic (minced)
- One teaspoon of salt
- Two teaspoons of chili powder
- One teaspoon of ground black pepper
- Two teaspoons of ground cumin
- Two teaspoons of ground cayenne pepper
- One tablespoon of honey
- One-fourth teaspoon of cinnamon
- Twelve ounces of kidney beans with liquid
- Twelve ounces of diced tomatoes with juice
- Two carrots (chopped)
- One green bell pepper (chopped)
- One bunch of green onions (chopped)
- One bunch cilantro (chopped)
- Eight ounces of dairy sour cream

Directions

- Keep the texturized vegetable protein in water and soak for thirty minutes. Press to drain.
- Over medium heat, heat oil in a pot and saute textured vegetable protein, onion and garlic until onion is soft and TVP browns evenly.
- Use salt, pepper, half of the chili powder, half of the cumin, half of the cayenne pepper and cinnamon to season.
- Combine in honey, beans, tomatoes, green bell pepper and carrots. For about fifty minutes, cook, turning from time to time.
- Use the rest of the chili powder, cumin and cayenne pepper to season. Keep on cooking for another fifteen minutes.
- Share into bowls, garnish using green onions and cilantro and then add a spoonful of sour cream on top before serving.

QUICK MANHATTAN CLAM CHOWDER

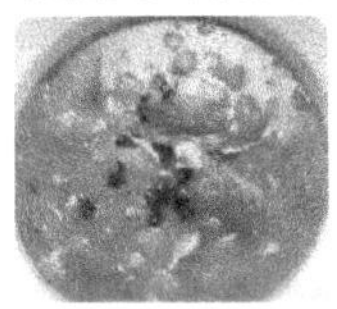

Servings: 8

Ingredients:

- One onion (diced)
- Four ribs celery (diced)
- One tablespoon of olive oil
- Sixteen ounces of baby carrots (diced)
- One clove garlic (minced)
- One tablespoon of chopped fresh basil
- Three cans of stewed tomatoes
- Black pepper
- Six and half ounces of minced calms (undrained)
- Two bottles clam juice
- Fourteen and half ounces of potatoes (drained and diced)
- One dash Worcestershire sauce

Directions

- Over medium heat, heat olive oil in a large pot. For about ten minutes, cook and turn onion, celery, carrots, basil, garlic and black pepper until vegetables are soft.
- Transfer half of the vegetable mix to a blender.
- Put two cans of stewed tomatoes into the pot. Drain the remaining can and add to the blender. Blend vegetable and tomato mixture until it is smooth. Add pureed mixture in the pot with vegetables.
- Combine clams, clam juice and potatoes in the pot and bring to boil. Lower the heat and for about eighteen minutes, simmer soup until it heats through, then use Worcestershire sauce to season the soup

PALEO CHICKEN STEW

Servings: 6

Ingredients:

- One red onion (chopped)
- Two teaspoons of olive oil
- Two cloves garlic (minced)
- Two sweet potatoes (peeled and chopped)
- Two skinless, boneless chicken breast halves (cut into cubes)
- One cup of fresh spinach
- One pinch of crushed red pepper
- One pinch of paprika
- Sea salt to taste
- Half cup of chicken broth

Directions

- ➢ Over-medium-high heat, heat oil in a saucepan. For about five minutes, saute onion and garlic in hot oil until it is tender.
- ➢ Add in chicken, sweet potatoes, spinach, crushed red pepper, paprika and sea salt with onion and garlic in the sauce pan. Add in chicken broth into the saucepan to the make the mixture soup or stew-like as you want.

- Bring broth to a boil, lower the heat to medium-low and for about thirty minutes, simmer until the chicken is no longer pink in the center and the sweet potatoes are soft.

CAJUN CHCIKEN AND SAUSAGE GUMBO

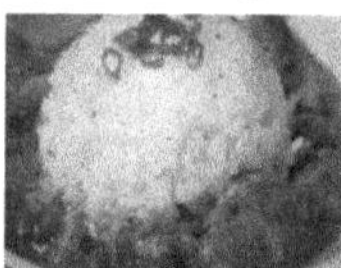

Servings: 10

Ingredients:

- One cup of all-purpose flour
- One cup of vegetable oil
- One onion (chopped)
- One green bell pepper (chopped)
- Two celery stalks (chopped)
- One pound of andouille or smoked sausage (sliced ¼ -inch thick)
- Four cloves garlic (minced)
- Salt and pepper
- Creole seasoning to taste
- Six cups of chicken broth
- One bay leaf

- One rotisserie chicken (boned and shredded)

Directions

- Over medium heat, heat oil in a Dutch oven. Once it gets hot beat in flour. Keep on whisking for about ten minutes until the roux cooked to chocolate milk color.
- Add in onion, bell pepper, celery and sausage into the roux. For about five minutes, cook. Put garlic and cook for more five minutes.
- Use salt, pepper and creole seasoning to season. Then blend very well.
- Add in chicken broth and bay leaf. Bring to boil over high heat, then lower the heat to medium-low and for an hour, simmer uncovered, turning from time to time. Add in chicken and simmer for additional one hour. During the last hour, skim off any floats to the top.

SPANISH –STYLE CHICKEN STEW

Servings: 4

Ingredients:

- Three red onions (cut into 1-inch cubes)
- Two tablespoons of olive oil
- Three cloves garlic (chopped)
- Twenty-eight ounces of Italian plum tomatoes
- Fifteen ounces of garbanzo beans
- Two cups of water
- One teaspoon of crushed red pepper flakes
- Two teaspoons of paprika
- Salt and pepper to taste
- Two carrots (cut into chunks)
- One potato (cubed)
- Four chicken thighs
- Four ounces of Spanish chorizo sausage (casing removed, sliced ¼ -inch thick)

Directions

- Over medium-high heat, heat olive oil in a saucepan. Add in onions and garlic, cook until the onion becomes tender and translucent. Add in tomatoes, garbanzo beans and water and season with paprika, red pepper flakes, salt and pepper. Add in carrots and potatoes, then keep chicken thighs skin-side up on top of the vegetables.
- Over high heat, bring to a boil then lower the heat to medium, cover and for about twenty-five minutes, simmer until the chicken is soft.
- Preheat oven to (400 degrees Fahrenheit).
- Bring the chicken out of the stew and keep aside. Add in the chorizo slices, then put the stew into glass baking dish. Keep the chicken thighs on top, skin-side up.
- For about fifteen minutes, bake in the preheated oven until the stew thickens and chicken crunchy.

SIDE DISH RECIPES

PUERTO RICAN TOSTONES (FRIED PLANTAINS)

Servings: 2

Ingredients:

- One green plantain
- Five tablespoons of oil (for frying)
- Three cups of cold water
- Salt to taste

Directions

- Peel plantain and slice into (1-inch chunks)
- Heat oil in a skillet and keep the plantains inside the oil. For about three minutes, fry per side on both sides.
- Bring out the plantain from the pan and flatten it by keeping a plate on the fried plantains and press it down.

- Immerse the plantains inside water, bring them back to hot oil and for minutes, fry on each side.
- Add salt and serve right away.

SUPERFAST ASPARAGUS

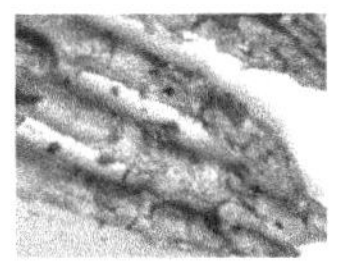

Servings: 3

Ingredients:

- One teaspoon of Cajun seasoning
- One pound of asparagus

Directions

- Preheat the oven to (425 degrees Fahrenheit).
- Snap asparagus at the softer part of the stalk and on a baking sheet, organize spears in one layer. Spray non-stick spray lightly and sprinkle Cajun seasoning.
- For about ten minutes, bake in the oven until soft.

AIR FRYER GARLIC AND PARSLEY BABY POTATOES

Servings: 4

Ingredients:

- One tablespoon of avocado oil
- One pound of baby potatoes (cut into quarters)
- One-fourth teaspoon of salt
- Half teaspoon of granulated garlic
- Half teaspoon of dried parsley

Directions

- ➢ Preheat air fryer to (350 degrees Fahrenheit).
- ➢ Mix potatoes and oil in a bowl and toss to coat. Put one-fourth teaspoon of granulated garlic and one-fourth teaspoon of parsley then toss to coat. Repeat with the rest of the garlic and parsley. Transfer potatoes into the air fryer basket.

- Keep the basket in the air fryer and for up to twenty minutes, cook and toss from time to time until it turns golden brown.

SAVORY ROASTED ROOT VEGETABLES

Servings: 6

Ingredients:

- Four carrots (diced)
- One cup of diced raw beet
- One onion (diced)
- Four cloves garlic (minced)
- Two cups of diced potatoes
- One-fourth cup of canned garbanzo beans (drained)
- Two tablespoons of olive oil
- One tablespoon of dried thyme leaves
- Salt and pepper to taste
- One-third cup of dry white wine
- One cup of torn beet greens

Directions

- Preheat oven to (400 degrees Fahrenheit).
- Keep the beet, carrot, onion, potatoes, garlic and garbanzo beans in a (9*13-inch) baking dish. Drizzle olive oil and use thyme, salt and pepper to season. Combine well.
- For about thirty minutes, bake, uncovered in the oven, turning once midway through baking. Take away the baking dish from the oven and for about fifteen minutes, bake until the wine evaporates and vegetables get soft. Add in the beet greens, let it wilt from the heat of the vegetables. Season with salt and pepper before you serve.

ROASTED ASPARAGUS WITH BASLMIC VINEGAR

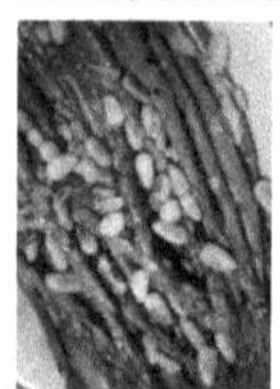

Servings: 6

Ingredients:

- Two tablespoons of olive oil
- Half pinch of ground sea salt
- Two pounds of fresh asparagus (trimmed)
- One-eight teaspoon of ground black pepper
- Three tablespoons of balsamic vinegar.

Directions

- Preheat oven to (400 degrees Fahrenheit).
- Keep the asparagus in a shallow (9*13-inch) baking dish. Sprinkle oil, salt and pepper, then toss to coat.
- For about eighteen minutes, bake in the oven until is turns light brown.
- Drizzle vinegar before you serve it.

EASY APPLE COLESLAW

Servings: 6

Ingredients:

- One unpeeled granny smith apple (cored and chopped)
- Three cups of chopped cabbage
- One unpeeled red apple (cored and chopped)
- One carrot (grated)
- Two green onions (chopped)
- Half cup of chopped red bell pepper
- One-third cup of mayonnaise
- One-third cup of brown sugar
- One tablespoon of lemon juice

Directions

- Mix cabbage. Red apple, green apple, carrot, red bell pepper and green onions in a bowl. In another bowl, combine mayonnaise, brown sugar and lemon juice and pour the dressing over salad.

EASY ROASTED POTATOES

Servings: 6

Ingredients:

- One teaspoon of McCorimick garlic powder
- One teaspoon of McCormick Dill weed
- Half teaspoon of salt
- Two pounds of red potatoes (slice into wedges)
- One-fourth teaspoon of McCormick black pepper (ground)
- One tablespoon of olive oil

Directions

- Preheat the oven to (400 degrees Fahrenheit).
- Combine dill weed, garlic powder, salt and pepper in a bowl. Keep aside.
- Use the oil in the bowl to toss potatoes and sprinkle the seasoning mix on the potatoes then toss to coat.
- On foil-lined (15*10*1-inch) baking pan, spread potatoes in a single layer

- For about thirty-five minutes, bake or until potatoes become soft and turn golden brown.

CRISPY BABY POTATOES

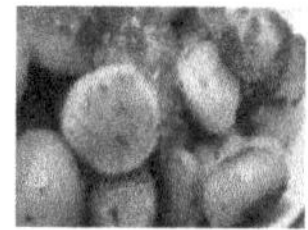

Servings: 4

Ingredients:

- Half teaspoon of dried parsley
- One-fourth teaspoon of garlic powder
- One and half pounds of baby potatoes (halved)
- Salt and ground black pepper to taste
- One tablespoon of olive oil

Directions

- Keep a steamer insert into a saucepan and fill with water just below the bottom of the steamer. Bring to a boil and put potatoes. Cover and for about eight minutes, steam until fork tender. It depends on the size of the potatoes.

- Pour the potatoes in a bowl. Put parsley, garlic, powder, salt and pepper and toss to coat.
- Over medium-high heat, heat oil in a skillet and put potatoes in the hot oil. Cook and shake the skillet from time to time until potatoes get browned on every side, taking up to eight minutes.

DESSERT RECIPES

LOW-FAT BROWNIES

Servings: 12

Ingredients:

- Six tablespoons of unsweetened cocoa powder
- Half cup of all-purpose flour
- One-eight teaspoon of salt
- One cup of white sugar
- Two tablespoons of vegetable oil
- Half teaspoon of vanilla extract

- One jar of pureed prunes baby food (four ounces)
- Two eggs

Directions

- ➢ Preheat oven to (350 degrees Fahrenheit) and grease (8*8 inch) square pan.
- ➢ Turn flour, cocoa, sugar and salt together in a bowl. Add in oil, vanilla, prunes and eggs. Combine until it blends well. Evenly spread the batter into the already set pan.
- ➢ For about thirty minutes, bake in the oven or until the up surface become shinny and inserted toothpick comes out neat.

LIMEABALEMON GLACIATE

Servings: 2

Ingredients:

- One ripe banana
- One and half cups of crushed ice
- Half lime (juiced)

- Half lemon (juiced)
- One tablespoon of shredded coconut (for garnishing)
- Two pitted cherries (for garnishing)

Directions

- In a blender set to low, blend together ice and banana until it mixes well. Put the lime juice and lemon juice while you blend to prevent the ice from freezing to the side of the blender.
- Use a tall glass to serve and garnish it with coconut or cherry.

STAWBERRIES WITH BALSAMIC VINEGAR

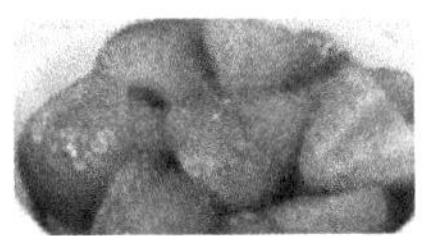

Servings: 6

Ingredients:

- Two tablespoons of balsamic vinegar

- Sixteen ounces of fresh strawberries (hulled and large berries cut in half)
- One-fourth cup of white sugar
- One-fourth teaspoon of freshly ground black pepper

Directions

- ➢ Keep strawberries in a bowl. Drizzle over with vinegar and sugar. Gently stir it to mix. Cover and allow sit at room temperature for not less than an hour but not greater than four hours.
- ➢ Grind pepper over berries before you serve.

HONEYSUCKLE PINEAPPLE

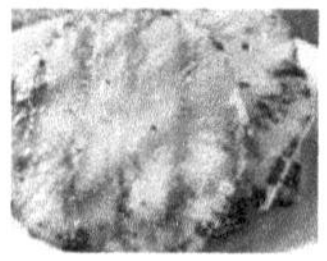

Servings: 6

Ingredients:

- One and half tablespoons honey
- Two tablespoons of cherry brandy
- Four slices fresh pineapple
- One teaspoon of lemon juice

Directions

- Preheat grill to medium heat and oil the grate lightly.
- Take away pineapple from the dish and discard any leftover marinade. Keep pineapple wedges right away on the rack or in a basket and for up to twelve minutes, grill. Turn as you grill until pineapple gets hot and caramelizes

AIR FRYER ROASTED BANANAS

Servings: 1

Ingredients:

- Avocado oil cooking spray
- One banana (cut into 1/8-inch thick diagonals)

Directions

- Use parchment paper to line air fryer basket.
- Preheat air fryer to (375 degrees Fahrenheit).

- Keep banana slices inside the basket and ensure that are not in contact with each other. Mist banana with avocado oil.
- Cook in the air fryer for about five minutes. Take away the basket and carefully turn over the banana slices. For about more three minutes, cook banana slices start to brown and caramelizes then remove from the basket.

BANANA AND PEANUT BUTTER 4-INGREDIENT ICE CREAM

Servings: 1

Ingredients:

- One teaspoon of confectioner`s sugar (not compulsory)
- Half teaspoon of milk
- Two slightly overripe bananas (cut into chunks)
- Two drops of vanilla extract
- One teaspoon of peanut butter

Directions

- Organize the banana chunks on a plate and for about two hours, freeze until solid.
- In blender, blend together frozen bananas, confectioner`s sugar, milk and vanilla extract until it becomes smooth and creamy. Put peanut butter and blend until smooth.

KILLER PUMPKIN PIE

Servings: 8

Ingredients:

Crust:

- Two tablespoons of all-purpose flour
- One and half cups of all-purpose flour plus
- Two teaspoons of white sugar
- One teaspoon of salt
- Half cup of canola oil
- Two tablespoons of rice milk

Filling:

- One-fourth cup of dark brown sugar
- Half cup of white sugar
- Two teaspoons of ground cinnamon
- Half teaspoon of salt
- Half teaspoon of ground ginger
- One-fourth teaspoon of ground nutmeg
- One-fourth teaspoon of ground cloves
- Fifteen ounces of pumpkin puree
- Two eggs
- Two tablespoons of canola oil
- One teaspoon of vanilla
- One and one-fourth cups of rice milk

Directions

- Preheat oven to (425 degrees Fahrenheit)
- Turn flour, sugar and salt together in (9-inch) pie pan and create a hole in the middle. Add in the oil and rice inside the hole and

combine using fork until a dough is formed. With hands, evenly press the mixture in the bottom and sides of the pan. Fold the edges of the crust.

- Turn the white sugar, brown sugar, cinnamon, salt, ginger, nutmeg and cloves together in a bowl. Keep aside. Beat together pumpkin puree, oil, eggs, vanilla and rice milk in another bowl until it blends evenly. Put the pumpkin mix to the dry ingredients and turn to blend well. Pour it in the prepared crust and keep on the cookie sheet in the oven.
- For about ten minutes, bake. Lower the temperature to (350 degrees Fahrenheit) and bake for up to forty-five minutes or until knife can come out neat when you insert it. Cool it on a metal rack.

GLUTEN FREE CRUSTLESS PUMPKIN PIE

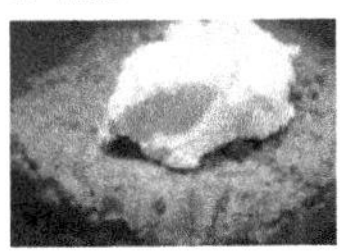

Servings: 8

Ingredients:

- Half cup of brown sugar
- Two eggs
- One teaspoon of ground cinnamon
- Half teaspoon of salt
- Half teaspoon of ground nutmeg
- One-fourth teaspoon of cloves
- One-eight teaspoon of ground ginger
- One and one-fourth cups of evaporated milk
- Fifteen ounces of can pumpkin puree
- One-fourth cup of chopped pecans (not compulsory)

Directions

- Preheat oven to (400 degrees Fahrenheit).
- In a bowl, whisk eggs, brown sugar, cinnamon, salt, nutmeg, cloves and ginger until they blend. Add in milk and pumpkin until the mixture gets smooth. Pour it in a

(9-inch) glass pie dish and then sprinkle pecans.

- For about fifteen minutes, bake in the oven and lower the heat to (350 degrees Fahrenheit) ad keep on baking for another thirty-five minutes or until it sets.
- For not less than an hour, cool and slice before you serve.

OVEN-FRIED BANANAS

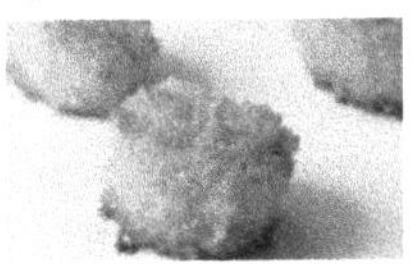

Servings:2

Ingredients:

- One-fourth cup of dry bread crumbs
- Cooking spray
- One tablespoon of granular no-calories sucralose sweetener, such as Splenda
- One-fourth teaspoon of ground cinnamon
- One-fourth teaspoon of ground ginger

- One pinch of salt
- One large banana (cut into slices)

Directions

- Preheat oven to (425 degrees Fahrenheit).
- Use parchment paper to line a baking sheet and spray with cooking spray.
- Mix bread crumbs, no-calories sweetener, cinnamon, ginger and salt in a bowl.
- Spray cooking spray on each side of the banana slices.
- Coat the banana slices with bread crumb mixture by rolling it in the mixture. Spray the slices once more with cooking spray.
- For about twelve minutes, bake on the oven or until crunchy.

CRUSTLESS PUMPKIN PIE

Servings: 8

Ingredients:

- One and one-fourth cups of skim milk
- Fifteen ounces of pumpkin puree
- Three-quarter cup of granular sucralose sweetener, such as Splenda
- Half cup of egg substitute
- One teaspoon of vanilla extract
- One teaspoon of ground cinnamon
- Half teaspoon of ground ginger
- Half teaspoon of ground nutmeg

Directions

- ➢ Preheat oven to (350 degrees Fahrenheit) and then grease a pie dish.
- ➢ Whisk pumpkin puree, milk, sweetener, egg substitute, vanilla extract, cinnamon, ginger and nutmeg in a bowl until smooth. Transfer into the prepared pie dish.
- ➢ For about thirty minutes, bake in the oven until it is set.

www.ingramcontent.com/pod-product-compliance
Ingram Content Group UK Ltd.
Pitfield, Milton Keynes, MK11 3LW, UK
UKHW021655190726
13853UKWH00001B/273